A Study Guide for
Contemporary Non-Western Cultures

(Anthropology 100)

Seventh Edition

Dorothy I. Davis
University of North Carolina Greensboro

Kendall Hunt
publishing company

Cover image © Shutterstock, Inc.

Kendall Hunt
p u b l i s h i n g   c o m p a n y

www.kendallhunt.com
Send all inquiries to:
4050 Westmark Drive
Dubuque, IA 52004-1840

Copyright © 1996, 1998, 2001, 2006, 2008, 2011, 2017 by Dorothy I. Davis

ISBN 978-1-5249-1334-2

Printed in the United States of America
10 9 8 7 6 5 4 3 2 1

CONTENTS

A NOTE TO THE STUDENT

This study guide was written especially for students in Anthropology 100, Contemporary Non-Western Cultures. In the late 1980s, the Anthropology Department decided to create a course appropriate for all students from freshmen to seniors. This course would serve to introduce students to the field of Anthropology and the Anthropology Department at UNC Greensboro, as well as offering three hours of Global/Non-Western and Social and Behavioral Science credits.

I realize that the three hours of G/N and/or SBS credit is the reason that most of you are taking this course, but hopefully you will enjoy ATY 100, and will continue to take other courses in Anthropology or related fields. This course includes a variety of articles from many different sources and introduces a perspective and approach to learning that you may not have been exposed to in high school. I believe that the course content is very applicable to the post 9-11 world that we live in today. The course addresses the important issues including ethnocentrism and cultural relativity, modernization, commercialization, and religious revitalization and fundamentalism.

In order to facilitate your learning, I have edited a textbook and now a workbook. This study guide covers all aspects of the course, including lectures, films, and tests, as well as the text. So if you do your reading, come to class and use this study guide, you should be able to handle anything that I decide to throw at you.

What I hope that you achieve by the end of the course is to develop a way of thinking. Some of you will have acquired this already, and you will just breeze through the course. Others will have more difficulty. One of the major problems for freshman students is *not* having the ability to "see the forest, through the trees." Through lectures, readings, and films you will be introduced to many interesting examples and illustrations (the trees). These are easy to remember. What is more difficult to understand is where they fit into themes and theories (the forest). You can learn a lot of facts and information but this is no advantage if you cannot put them into context.

The goal of this study guide is to help you to learn to distinguish between what is important and what is trivial, and then to understand how the important things interrelate. This is knowledge that should help you not only through this course, but through your college career and your life as well. On completing this course, students should be able to: 1. demonstrate how many diverse societies are increasingly interconnected ans interdependent in the modern world, 2. have an understanding of the concepts of ethnocentrism, cultural relativity, and human rights, 3. develop a sense of tolerance and understanding toward the problems faced by indigenous people in the world today, 4. challenge the Eurocentric view of world history.

INTRODUCTION TO THE STUDY GUIDE

Both the course and the study guide are divided into four units. Unit I introduces the course and the field of Anthropology. This unit lasts approximately four to five weeks. Units II and III will cover different geographical and cultural areas. In Unit II, we will start with a study of the native peoples of North America. As the guide will still be introducing some anthropological terms and concepts, we will spend about three weeks in this section. Unit II will finish with two weeks of studying native peoples of South America. In Unit III, we will spend two weeks each studying Africa and Oceania. In the final unit we learn about the "Tasmanian Extinction". Genocide is the worst thing that can happen when two cultures come into contact with each other. The contact history of the West with Japan varies greatly from the patterns of contact that we have studied so far this semester. In the last class meetings, I will briefly review the whole semester and look more closely at the role of contemporary applied anthropology. There is a quiz at the end of each unit.

This study guide will help you to integrate the material that you will be getting from a variety of resources. Each unit is divided into about eight sections. The following is a description of each section and some brief study hints, if appropriate.

OVERVIEW

The overview is a short description of the subject matter covered in each unit.

LECTURE OUTLINE

I do not use Power Point slides in this class for two reasons. Power Point slides tend to compartmentalize learning. In this course, it is necessary to understand the sequence of events from the beginning of the unit until the end. The unit length outlines in this study guide will help you learn to do this. The second reason that I do not use Power Point slides is because one of the goals of this course is to teach students how to take notes. Students often have a problem with lecture notes. Although I give a lot of information in my lectures, they follow an outline form. I have not divided the outline by lecture, but by unit, because of varying class schedules. This is only a lecture *outline;* it does not replace taking notes in class. I would recommend that you look over the outline before you come to class. That way you will have some idea about what I will be talking about. Reviewing the outline after class to see if you missed something (comparing notes with other students is a good way to see what you have missed too) is advisable. Use the outlines to help highlight your notes so that you can distinguish the major topics from the examples. You may want to write your notes on just one side of the page and copy the appropriate lecture outline on the opposite page. This would provide a "boxed review," similar to those found in many textbooks. I have also made reference to the articles and the films in the notes. A starred notation with the author's name will appear in the outline where the articles are particularly relevant to the lecture. This should also help you stay current with your reading assignments. Finally, if you should fall asleep during class, the lecture outline will tell you what you missed!

KEY TERMS AND VOCABULARY

Some of these vocabulary lists will seem awfully long. Many of the terms listed are probably words that you already know, but be careful. Some terms, like "culture," may be used differently in general speech than in the academic discipline of Anthropology. If I define a word in class, make a note of this in the margins of your notes. Copy this definition into your workbook. Do not depend on Google for definitions for these terms. Definitions make easy test questions, both for you and for me. One of the weaknesses in the field of Anthropology is that we don't often agree on how to define terms. For example, there are over 100 definitions for the term "culture." In class, I define it as "way of life." Put that in your workbook and remember it. It's on the test. The vocabulary lists come mostly from lecture, but I have also included terms given in the readings that may be new to you. If you ever come across a term or concept that you don't understand, ask me about it.

GROUPS YOU SHOULD KNOW

These groups are usually societies or cultures that are mentioned in class, films, or readings. It is very likely that they will be referred to again throughout the semester. You should be able to tell me where these groups are, what distinguishes them from others, and the context in which they were mentioned. For example, in the beginning of the semester, we will talk about the Tiwi. Just noting that these are aboriginal people in Australia is not enough. The fact that they practiced an unusual (to us) form of marriage, and the Catholic priests attempted to convert them, is not enough. Why did I introduce them at this point? Check your outline and put them into a context. Their contact history provides a good example of cultural integration—one of the fundamental characteristics of culture. This is what I mean by being able to "see the forest for the trees."

MAPS AND/OR CHARTS

These are supplemental materials or learning aids. We often go over this material in class.

ARTICLE REVIEWS

It is important to do your reading before we discuss it in class. Being familiar with an article gives you an advantage when we discuss it in class. In this study guide, I will give a short description of the article and ask you some key questions. This should help you focus your reading, so refer to this section before and after you read the article. If you have been taught how to write a précis or abstract, this is the ideal way to study these articles. A précis is a thirty-to-forty word summary of the article. To study for the test, all you have to do is reread the précis, not the whole article. If you do not know how to write a précis, here are some helpful hints. Do not underline with a highlighter. All you will end up with are nicely colored pages. Use a pen and underline key phrases and terms. Make notes in the margins. When you start to read an article, look carefully at the title; it should give you a clue as to what the article is about. Don't forget the subtitles either. Then read the first paragraph and the last paragraph. The author should have told you in the first paragraph what he/she is trying to show you, and in the conclusion, what he/she did show you. If the article is broken into sections, with distinct topics, this should serve as an outline. Be aware of what you are reading, and look for a point of view, a proposition, and supporting arguments. We can all sit down, spend a half-hour mindlessly reading fifteen pages, and have no clue about what we read when we finished. If you make notes in the margins, or write one descriptive sentence for each page, you will become a disciplined reader, learn more, and learn easier. Your time is valuable—you need to learn to make the most of it.

FILM REPORT

Films are a very important learning tool in Anthropology. They enable us to visit a culture for a short period of time. The films I have chosen are related to the course material. Before showing a film, the culture described, and the reason I'm showing it. Make a note of this and transfer it to your workbook. I think it is good practice to take notes during the film, as this helps you to stay focused. There are usually one or two test questions on each film, and they tend to be very general.

SAMPLE TEST QUESTIONS

I've written up some questions that are similar to those that you will find on the quizzes. Most classes have 50–120 students, so the test format is multiple choice. However, all make-up tests are a combination of short answer and essay, so I have included both in the study guide. It will not hurt you to look at both types of questions to help you to prepare for either type of quiz. You will see what kind of information that I'm looking for. In making up a multiple-choice test, I start with the correct answer in mind, and a foil (i.e. "Close, but no cigar"). Be forewarned, I've been known to get a little silly on my other choices. However, in Anthropology, the silly sounding answers are often the correct ones. Some questions are straight-forward. Others are reasoning questions; they draw on your thinking skills. When we go over the tests in class, try to understand why you answered a question wrong. If you picked the foil, you are better off than if you had picked a ridiculous answer. If you missed a fact question, you are doing worse than if you miss a more difficult reasoning question. Let me make a point about the "All of the above" and "None of the above" questions. For the former, if you find two answers that you are sure of, go with "All of the above." The "None of the above" questions are harder. Don't try to twist a statement into being true just to avoid the "None of the above" answer.

For essay tests and short answer tests, read the question carefully and answer *all* parts. Rather than just writing down what you know, answer the question. The more sources you can incorporate into your answers (even information from other courses), the better your grade will be. *Note:* You may have noticed the study guide does not include the answers to practice questions. I believe that you will learn more if you have to go back to your sources to research and find the correct answer.

TEST REVIEW

We cover a lot of material in each unit. Use this as a study guide. Make up note cards. Study with a friend. Just remember, context, context (forest), and context! Test reviews list the items on the test that come from the lectures. If correctly answered, the article reviews will prepare you well for the readings section of the quizzes. The best way to prepare for the test questions is to find the terms listed in the review in your notes, so that you can see them in context. For example you may remember what the post-partum sex taboo is, but make sure that you are able to relate it to the topics of ethnocentrism and cultural relativity. Your course outline section in each unit should help you do this.

This is obviously an incomplete review of study skills. There are many books on the subject, and the Office of Academic Advising offers study skills sessions each semester. These courses or books can really help you maximize your grades and minimize your study time. There are also tutors for this course available at the Student Success Center. They are well worth the extra time that you put into them. If you are having trouble in my course, you can always make an appointment to come and see me. If you're not doing the reading, not coming to class, and cannot understand why you are failing, I cannot help you. But, if you are really trying and not doing well, you need to see me *as soon as possible*. Do not wait until after you have failed all of the quizzes. There is no extra credit in this course, except the extra credit quiz questions (6 points for each test). After spending some time with this workbook, you should learn a lot, get a good grade, and be a happy camper!

UNIT I

AN INTRODUCTION TO THE COURSE AND THE FIELD OF ANTHROPOLOGY

OVERVIEW

Unit I introduces both this course and the discipline of Anthropology. Anthropologists study human beings from any time and place. We will narrow this field of investigation down to the time period from 1500 to the present. After Columbus's first voyage in 1492, the subsequent expansion of European states had a big impact on the rest of the world. Many Western and non-Western cultures came into contact with each other for the first time. When this happened, *both* cultures changed. Most of you have studied these events from the Western or Eurocentric point of view. In this course, we will attempt to understand these contact situations from the perspective of the people in the non-Western cultures. These historical events have shaped the modern world, so we will move quickly to studies of contemporary societies and issues while continuing to emphasize the natives' point of view. You may not always agree with this perspective, but you should begin to understand why others do not always see us as we see ourselves.

Anthropology is the perfect discipline in which to take this approach. In this section, I will introduce you to the field of Anthropology including its subdisciplines, its methodology, the study of culture, and culture change.

LECTURE OUTLINE—AN INTRODUCTION TO THE COURSE AND THE FIELD OF ANTHROPOLOGY

I. Introduction to the course

  A. Time frame—1500 to the present

  B. Areas covered
    1. North America
    2. South America
    3. Africa
    4. Oceania
    5. Japan

II. Themes, Points of View and Perspectives in Anthropology

  A. Holism
    1. Chronology/European Expansion
      a. Cultural Factors
      b. Geographical Factors
    2. Clash of Cultures and Ripple Effect   *Fagan

  B. Bias and Prejudice   *Map I a + b
    1. Maps
    2. Columbus Poster

  C. Globalization
    1. Guinea Worms
    2. Clothing

  D. Double Standards/Hypocrisy
    1. Headhunters
      a. Jivaro
      b. Maori

III. Introduction to the field of Anthropology

  A. Definition—Scientific study of humankind

  B. History

  C. 4 (5) Subdisciplines of Anthropology
    1. Physical or biological
      a. Human variation
      b. Human evolution

  2. Linguistics
   a. Language and culture
   b. Evolution and language
   c. Glottochronology
  3. Archaeology/Archeology
   a. Material objects
   b. Prehistoric
   c. Historic
  4. Cultural Anthropology
   a. Universal Unilineal Evolution
   b. Ethnography and ethnology
  5. Applied Anthropology   *Plotkin

IV. Method in Anthropology

 A. Holistic approach
  1. Fieldwork
  2. Team fieldwork/participant observation   *Cornish
   a. Ethics   *Film: Yanomamo

 B. Comparative approach
  1. Examples
   a. Lines and angles
   b. Food
   c. Gestures
  2. Ethnocentrism
   a. Concepts of beauty
   b. Anthropologists and ethnocentrism in the field   *Miner
    1) Tony Whitehead
  3. Cultural relativism and human rights
   a. Post-partum sex taboo
   b. Honor Killings

 C. Concept of culture
  1. A way of life
  2. Fundamental characteristics

V. Fundamental characteristics of culture

 A. Culture is uniquely human
  1. Protoculture/almost culture

 B. Culture includes everything and the parts are integrated   *Film: Yanomamo
  1. Yanomamo
  2. Tiwi

C. Culture is learned by each member of a society during his/her socialization
    1. Enculturation
    2. Acculturation

D. Culture provides humans with a way of satisfying their biological and emotional needs in a manner approved by society
    1. Biological needs/drives
        a. Food, warmth, shelter
        b. Reproduction
    2. Socialization
    3. Production and distribution of goods
    4. Maintaining order
    5. Meaning for life and motivation

E. Culture is always changing
    1. Different rates
    2. Examples
        a. Medical technology and ethics
        b. Kids' songs

VI. How and why cultures change

  A. Discovery

  B. Invention

  C. Diffusion

  D. Acculturation

  E. Rebellion and revolt

  F. Culture loss

VII. Culture change in the modern world

  A. Commercialization
    1. Migratory labor
    2. Non-agricultural commercial production
    3. Supplementary cash crops
    4. Industrialized agriculture

  B. Modernization
    1. Four subprocesses
    2. Modernization and ethnocentrism
    3. First, Second, Third, Fourth World

C. Religious revitalization
   1. Handsome Lake
   2. Cargo cults
      a. John Frumm
      b. LBJ
   3. Fundamentalism

D. Globalization/Localization   *Bestor

E. Voice and Agency   *Mankiller

KEY TERMS AND VOCABULARY

Chronological

Clash of cultures

Perspective

Subdiscipline

Linguistics

Glottochronology

Universal Unilineal Evolution

Ethnography

Ethnology

Holistic

Participant observation

Ethnocentrism

Cultural relativity

Culture

Protoculture

Socialization

Enculturation

Acculturation

Discovery

Invention

Diffusion

Commercialization

Modernization

First, Second, Third, Fourth World

Globalization

Localization/Indigenization

Religious revitalization

Cargo cults

Infanticide

Post-partum sex taboo

Shaman

Multiculturalism

Genocide

Progress

Pluralism

Indigenous people

Applied anthropology

Intellectual Property Rights

Honor Killings

GROUPS YOU SHOULD KNOW

Maori

Tiwi

Yanomamo

Nacirema

Handsome Lake

John Frumm

LBJ cult

People without a history

ARTICLE REVIEWS

Brian Fagan: *Clash of Cultures*
                   "Introduction and Prologue"

Brian Fagan, an archeologist, wrote a book entitled *Clash of Cultures,* which deals with the expansion of European states and what happened when Western and non-Western cultures came into contact with each other for the first time. This book covers the same geographical areas as this course, so Fagan's Prologue is a good introduction to this course and it's subject matter. After reading these pages, you should be able to answer the following questions:

• What does Fagan mean by the phrases *"clash of cultures"* and the *"ripple effect"?*

• What point of view does Fagan emphasize?

• What was the natives' perspective of European expansion?

• Why did some societies survive contact and actually prosper, while others disappeared?

- Who are the "people without a history?

Andrew Cornish: *"Participant Observation on a Motorcycle"*

Cornish is an anthropologist who has written an amusing, tongue-in-cheek, self-deprecatory account of what he learned about adjudicating disputes in Thailand after a motorcycle accident.

- You could call this incident "fieldwork by accident". Why?

- How was the case settled? Was "fault" an issue? What role was played by the witnesses?

- What two ethnographic mistakes did Cornish admit that he made?

Horace Minor: *"Body Ritual Among the Nacirema"*

Even though this article is over 50 years old, it is still included in introductory Anthropology courses. It was the first of many articles about the Nacirema. Many anthropology students have actually written Nacirema articles since they are intimately familiar with this peculiar culture.

- Who are the Nacirema?

- What is the point of view of this article?

- Does the anthropological jargon make this culture seem more primitive than it actually is?

- How does this relate to both historical and contemporary accounts written about other cultures?

Mark J. Plotkin: *"Shamans"*

Mark Plotkin is an ethnobotanist who has studied shamans in the Amazon region of South America. In this article he relates his experiences and those of other westerners with medicine men and women throughout the world. He looks at both the medical and spiritual aspects of shamanism, its origins in human history as well as what shamans have to contribute to modern medicine.

- What is ayahuasca? What was Plotkin's experience with the drug? Could you classify this as an example of participant observation? Why?

- Why is Plotkin in South America searching for healing plants? What's the urgency?

- What are "intellectual property rights"? "Rape and run"? How do these concepts apply to Plotkin's work?

- How did shamans learn which plants have medical properties? Include the 5 reasons given in the article with the 1 added by your professor?

Shoefoot (Batista Cajicuwa): *"New Spirits for Old"*

This article provides a good example of acculturation. The Yanomami Shaman, Shoefoot, has been converted to Christianity by Evangelical missionaries. He now sees his traditional culture through their eyes and recounts how much better off he and his people are today.

- Who is Shoefoot? What are the Old Spirits? The New?

- Why did he become dissatisfied with his own culture?

Wilma Mankiller: *"Being Indigenous in the 21st Century"*

- The author writes that Indigenous Peoples all have three things in common. What are they?

- She states that it is almost impossible for "outsiders" to understand the issues faced by Indigenous Peoples today?

- Who are the outsiders to whom she is referring? How does the anthropologist fit in with all of this?

- What does she state is the most common misconception about Indigenous Peoples?

- Does Mankiller see hope for the future of Indigenous peoples? What do they need to do in order to survive?

Theodore C. Bestor: *How Sushi Went Global"*

Bestor writes about both the business and cultural aspects of globalization. He focuses on both the complicated international markets, regulations, ecological impact, etc. associated with the blue fin tuna trade and with its status as a Japanese cultural property.

- Why is the tuna trade a great example of the globalization of a regional industry?

- How does tuna fishing differ on the two sides of the Atlantic Ocean? What is the environmental impact?

- How does sushi still retain its status as a Japanese cultural property despite globalization?

- What do you think the Japanese would think of our "Chicken of the Sea" Advertizing slogan for tuna?

FILM REPORT

The Yanomamo: A Multidisciplinary Study

- What is the main idea of this video?

- List important facts used to support the main idea.

- How does this video relate to your readings and the lecture?

PRACTICE TEST QUESTIONS

Multiple Choice

1. This is the subdiscipline of Anthropology that studies material objects to help understand about human culture.
   a. Physical Anthropology
   b. Cultural Anthropology
   c. Archaeology
   d. Linguistics
   e. Epidemiology

2. "We are best" is a description of which way of thinking?
   a. ethnocentrism
   b. cultural relativity
   c. egocentrism
   d. homocentrism
   e. none of the above

3. To prevent Kwaspakior, a protein deficiency disease, women in the tropics should:
   a. take vitamin supplements.
   b. eat insects and fungus.
   c. continue to nurse their infants through their rapid growth period.
   d. commit male infanticide.
   e. be promiscuous.

4. Catholic priests were able to convert the Tiwi of Australia after they convinced the aborigines that they would go to Hell for marrying infant girls.
   a. true
   b. false

5. The discussion of the fieldwork experience of Tony Whitehead showed:
   a. how anthropologists usually hide their real identity when in the field.
   b. even anthropologists can be susceptible to ethnocentrism.
   c. how lonely academics can find a spouse in the field.
   d. how two anthropologists abandoned Western culture and decided to live with the people they were studying.
   e. how easy it is to do participant observation.

6. Patrick Tierney accuses Chagnon and Neel of
   a. causing and epidemic of measles among the Yanomamo
   b. destroying manioc crops in western Brazil
   c. introducing firearms to the Kayapo
   d. encouraging single women to commit infanticide
   e. all of the above

7. According to Ralph Linton the impact of diffusion on American culture is
   a. 20%
   b. 30%
   c. 50%
   d. 75%
   e. 90%

8. Developing countries are referred to as:
   a. First World.
   b. Second World.
   c. Third World.
   d. Fourth World.
   e. Under World

Matching

9. _____ Cherokee
10. _____ LBJ Cult
11. _____ Cornish
12. _____ Yanomamo
13. _____ Huron

a. motorcycle
b. Mankiller
c. female infanticide
d. Cargo Cults
e. felt hats

Multiple Choice

14. The world's oldest profession is (Re: Plotkin) _____.
    a. prostitution
    b. shamanism
    c. politicians
    d. drug dealers
    e. anthropologists

15. In the film *The Yanomamo*, we saw this expert at work in the field.
    a. anthropologist
    b. dentist
    c. linguist
    d. geneticist
    e. all of the above

16. Which of the following is NOT an example of the globalization of sushi?
    a. Environmental regulations about how to legally catch tuna vary between the US and Europe.
    b. Sushi is popular in Chinese restaurants
    c. Graduates of the Sushi Daigaku can use their certificates to get good paying jobs in Japan.
    d. Fish caught in New England are sent to Japan to be cut up and then the pieces are sent back to high end restaurants in New York City.
    e. Tuna can swim as fast as 50 mph and can cross the Atlantic Ocean in two months.

Short Answer

1. List the five fundamental characteristics of culture.

2. What is meant by the holistic and comparative approach in Anthropology? How do these approaches distinguish Anthropology from the other behavioral sciences?

3. What did Andrew Cornish learn about settling, disputes in Thailand after his motor cycle accident? Have you ever been involved in a traffic accident? Was the outcome the same or different?

4. What three things does Wilma Mankiller say that all Indigenous People have in common?

5. Explain why I have used Plotkin's article as an example of ethnocentrism? How does it compare to the Nacirema?

Essay

1. Why did some societies survive contact when others did not? (Fagan) List the reasons and then compare the experiences of two different groups of people.

2. What is culture loss? Using the lecture and the readings, discuss why we should be concerned about this today.

3. Define ethnocentrism and cultural relativism. Under which circumstances are they (1) desirable; (2) undesirable? Illustrate.

4. Compare Shoefoot's life history to that of the Yanomamo you saw in the film. What does the anthropologist, Kenneth Good, think about Shoefoot's conversion? Does this happen often?

5. What does Fagan mean by the Terms, "Clash of Cultures" and "Ripple Effect"? Give a detailed example.

6. Using the Tiwi describe the cultural integration.

7. What does Mankiller mean when she talks about a strong sense of community among native peoples?

REVIEW FOR QUIZ #1—AN INTRODUCTION TO THE COURSE AND THE FIELD OF ANTHROPOLOGY

4 (5) subdisciplines of ATY

Definition of culture (4 words)

Holistic approach

Comparative method

Nacirema

Fundamentals of culture

Ethnocentrism

Cultural relativity

Whitehead

Post-partum sex taboo

Tiwi

Globalization

Localization

Types of culture change

Cargo Cults—Handsome Lake

Clash of cultures—Fagan definition

Ripple effect

Point of view of Fagan

Diffusion

Acculturation

Enculturation

Yanomamo

Commercialization

Religious revitalization

Modernization

Pluralism

Multidisciplinary studies

Visual perception (example)

Chagnon vs. Tierney

Culture

Protoculture

First, Second, Third, Fourth World

Ethics in ATY

Articles (@ 2 questions each)

Film: *The Yanomamo: A Multidisciplinary Study*

UNIT II

NORTH AMERICA
AND SOUTH AMERICA

OVERVIEW

The next two units will cover specific geographical areas. For each area, we will first look at the ecological and cultural diversity at contact. We will then trace the history and the impact of contact for contemporary populations.

There are two reasons why this unit features North and South America. The first reason is that these areas are the most familiar to us, since this is where we live. The second reason is chronological. Europeans colonized the New World hundreds of years before they were able to make much of an impact on either Africa or Oceania.

The first lectures in this unit will deal with both North and South America. Using map IIA as a base we will explore the geographical and cultural diversity of the New World before European contact. I will also briefly introduce some of the theories about how the New World was originally settled by Native Americans. Many of the established theories are being challenged by new lines of evidence. Even though these theories were proposed by archeologists, they have a political impact for contemporary American Indians.

In the section on North America, you will be introduced to more terms and concepts central to anthropology. An understanding of adaptation is basic to this course. Humans adapt both biologically and culturally to their environments. The disease factor is a good example of biological and cultural elements influencing each other. The disease factor plays an important role in contact history.

Another important concept is that of the cultural area. This concept was developed by American anthropologists studying Native American cultures. It has been successfully applied to other areas as well.

We will look briefly at the post contact history and the range of policies toward native peoples, including the conflicting policies of assimilation and pluralism, issues of sovereignty, and the characteristics that make Native Americans a distinct minority in this country today.

In our discussion of South America, I will use maps, the concept of culture area, and a model of change to explain cultural diversity before contact, what happened at contact, and what the contemporary status of the native people is today.

LECTURE OUTLINE—NORTH AMERICA

I. North America and South America

    A. Cultural and Geographic Diversity at contact
        1. Language
        2. Geography
        3. Culture

    B. Migration from Asia to the New World   *Map 1a
        1. Old and New theories
            a. who
            b. when
            c. where
        2. Native's views

    C. Culture areas   *Map IIb
        1. Adaptation
            a. Disease   *Diamond
                1) Impact rate
                2) Why little or no resistance to Old World diseases for New World populations
                3) Smallpox
                4) Syphilis

    D. Assimilation
        1. Training schools   *Film
        2. Vanishing Indians   *Dobkins

    E. Pluralism

    F. Indian population trends
        1. United States
        2. Canada
        3. Mexico

    G. Controversial Issues for First Nations
        1. Peyote
        2. Mascots
        3. Advertising

    H. Indian Stereotyping
        1. Awareness Inventory   *Chart IIc
        2. What It Means to Be Indian
        3. Historic/Contemporary Indian

   I. Gaming

   J. Indian contributions
- **1.** Food
  - **a.** Potato
  - **b.** Maize
  - **c.** Manioc
  - **d.** Others
- **2.** Drugs
- **3.** Clothing and furniture
- **4.** Art
- **5.** Language
- **6.** White Shamanism
- **7.** Government

II. North America—Contemporary Perspective

   A. What makes Indians a distinct minority in the United States
- **1.** Immigration
- **2.** Legislative history

   B. Indians and Racism
- **1.** Discrimination
- **2.** Differences in Civil Rights movement for African Americans and Native Americans

   C. Most administered minority
- **1.** Independent sovereign nations
- **2.** Domestic dependent sovereign nations
- **3.** Franchise 1924
- **4.** Land Claims Court
  - **a.** Maine
  - **b.** Nunavut   *Bodley

   D. Summary of Indian policy of U.S. government
- **1.** Assumptions/Paternalism
- **2.** Forced assimilation
- **3.** Directed acculturation
- **4.** Contradictions in Policy

   E. Distinctive ways that Indians relate to larger white-dominated society
- **1.** X
- **2.** Y   **Little Finger
- **3.** Z

F. Goals of Indians today
1. Education
2. Preservation of language, culture, and tradition
3. Health
4. Others

*Lake

KEY TERMS AND VOCABULARY

Native American

First Nations Peoples

Indian

1492—Impact date

New World

Western Hemisphere

Foraging

Immigration

Emigration

Culture area

Adaptation

Subsistence levels

Bering Straits

Land bridge

Agriculture

Horticulture

Homo sapiens

Animal vectors of disease

Assimilation

Forced assimilation

Carlisle School

George Pratt

Corporations and Bands

Chairperson/chief

Reservation

Half-breed/métis/mestizo

Peyote

Native American Church

Nunavut

Percaps

Nation

Indigenous

Sovereignty

Independent Sovereign Nations

Domestic Dependent Sovereign Nations

Directed acculturation

Red Power

Apples and radishes

Russell Means

Dennis Banks

XYZ Indians

Federal paternalism

Individualism vs. communalism

Maize

Manioc

Patrilineal/matrilineal

Wounded Knee

BIA

AIM

GROUPS YOU SHOULD KNOW

Kiowa (Legend of Uncle Saynday)

Cherokee

Lumbee

Passamaquoddy and Penobscot

League of the Iroquois

Navaho

Hopi

Lakota/Sioux/People of the Seven Council Fires

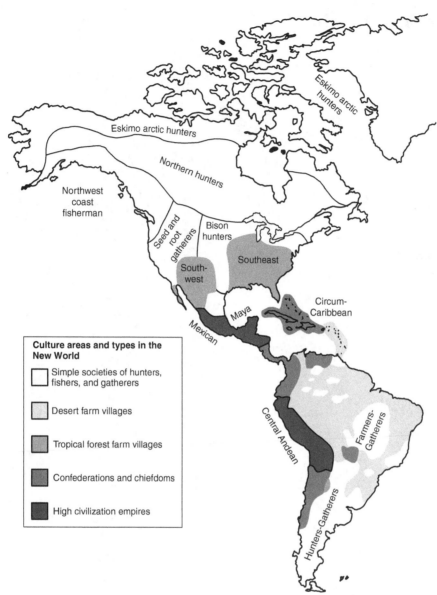

Map IIA
© Kendall Hunt Publishing Company

Culture areas and types in the New World

☐ Simple societies of hunters, fishers, and gatherers

Desert farm villages

Tropical forest farm villages

Confederations and chiefdoms

High civilization empires

Eskimo arctic hunters

Eskimo arctic hunters

Northern hunters

Northwest coast fisherman

Seed and root gatherers

Bison hunters

Southeast

South-west

Maya

Mexican

Circum-Caribbean

Central Andean

Farmers-Gatherers

Hunters-Gatherers

Teaching About Native Americans   **CHART IIC**

INDIAN AWARENESS INVENTORY

DIRECTIONS: Circle the letter that represents what you know to be true (T) or false (F). If you are unsure of the answer, circle unsure (U). This is a personal inventory developed to help you determine your knowledge about Native Americans. Do not try to guess.

	TRUE	FALSE	UNSURE
1. *Since many Indian people live close to nature, they tend to be healthier than non-Indians.*	T	F	U
2. *Most Indians are proud of being Indian.*	T	F	U
3. Most Indian men do not need to shave.	T	F	U
4. *Most Indians receives free hospitalization.*	T	F	U
5. *Because of past treaties, Indian people do not have to register for the Armed Forces.*	T	F	U
6. *Indian people have the highest suicide rate of any group in the country.*	T	F	U
7. *Most Indian people do not pay taxes.*	T	F	U
8. On the majority of reservations, Indian people need permission to leave.	T	F	U
9. Many Indian men still refer to their wives as squaws.	T	F	U
10. The majority of all Indian families carry water one mile or more to their homes.	T	F	U
11. *Indian tribes are culturally deprived in some parts of the country.*	T	F	U
12. Indians originated the practice of scalping their enemies.	T	F	U
13. *Most Indian children attend Bureau of Indian Affairs schools.*	T	F	U
14. Most Indians are carefree and happy people.	T	F	U
15. Because of religious beliefs, many Indians do not carry insurance.	T	F	U
16. Indians use the phrase "low man on the totem pole" to refer to a person in a group who has the lowest status.	T	F	U
17. Most Indians have high cheekbones.	T	F	U
18. *Some Indians are still Indian givers.*	T	F	U
19. In some states, Indian people are not to vote in elections.	T	F	U
20. Twenty percent of Indian families have no houses of their own.	T	F	U
21. Because of conflicting values, Indian people tend to have a high rate of failure in business.	T	F	U
22. *Indians are usually good hunters.*	T	F	U
23. *The academic achievement level of most Indian children is below that of white children.*	T	F	U

	TRUE	FALSE	UNSURE
24. Because of their sense of direction, Indian people who come to the city can find their way around.	T	F	U
25. *Indian people tend to be good farmers because of their reverence for the land.*	T	F	U
26. *In the last 75 years, Indians have lost over 40 percent of their land.*	T	F	U
27. Indian athletes tend to be long-distance runners rather than sprinters.	T	F	U
28. *Most tribes still have chiefs.*	T	F	U
29. *A person who is one-fifth Indian is called a "half-breed."*	T	F	U
30. *Indians tend to die younger than non-Indians.*	T	F	U
31. An Indian man received a war bonnet when he became a chief.	T	F	U
32. *The majority of Indian youth drop out of school by the tenth grade.*	T	F	U
33. *Because of genetic factors, many Indian people are alcoholics.*	T	F	U
34. Some Indians get funds from the United States government for living on a reservation.	T	F	U
35. *Fewer than 5 percent of Indian children have an Indian teacher.*	T	F	U
36. Many Indian men make good auto mechanics because of their experience with arts and handicrafts.	T	F	U
37. *Indians comprise less than 1 percent of the total population of the United States.*	T	F	U
38. *President Nixon stated publicly that Native Americans are the most deprived and isolated group in our nation.*	T	F	U
39. *The average income of Indian Americans is $1,500 a year.*	T	F	U
40. *There are laws that prohibit Indian people from drinking alcoholic beverages.*	T	F	U

"Appendix A: Indian Awareness Inventory," from *Teaching About Native Americans,* by Karen D. Harvey, Lisa D. Harjo, and Jane K. Jackson, Bulletin #84, 1990, pp. 74–75. © National Council for the Social Studies. Reprinted by permission.
INSTRUMENT DEVELOPED BY: John Fletcher (Blackfoot), Church Ross (Lakota), and Gary Kush (non-Indian).

ARTICLE REVIEWS

Jared Diamond: *"The Arrow of Disease"*

Jared Diamond is a popular writer who often takes a different perspective on history. In this article, he looks at the role that disease plays in the conquest of the New World. He focuses on the interaction of disease organisms with human biology and culture.

- What is an ideal environment from the point of the "bug" or "germs" that cause disease?

- Why are epidemic diseases sometimes called the "diseases of civilization"?

- What role do animals play as vectors of disease? Use bird flu as an example.

- Why did Native Americans have no resistance to many imported European diseases?

Rebecca Dobkins: *"Corresponding with Power: Letters between the mothers of California Indian children and the federal boarding-school officials, 1916-1922"*

We have learned about forced assimilation and Indian boarding schools in class ans film. Dobkins is writing about the Greenville Indian School in California. Her focus is on the power relationships between Indian families and the federal government.

- What experiences does Dobkin's have in her background that she feels makes her qualified to write an article about these letters?

- What does she mean by the term, resistance? What actions revealed in the letters can be identified as resistance?

- The boarding schools were designed to teach the Western value of _____ to replace the Indian value of _____. Can you relate this to Mankiller's article.

Robert Lake (Medicine Grizzlybear): *"An Indian Father's Plea"*

Medicine Grizzlybear is the father of a 5-year-old boy, Wind Wolf. His son is the only Native American child in his school, has no friends, has been diagnosed as learning disabled, and is embarrassed about being a Native American. The understandably concerned father writes a message to his son's teacher.

- What is the "plea" that Medicine Grizzlybear is making? What does he believe that the teacher can do to help his son?

- What type of "education" had Wind Wolf received before he went to school? What does his father mean when he states that his child is not "culturally disadvantaged, just culturally different"?

- What does the father want? What does the son want?

- How does the father's request relate to the concept of pluralism discussed in class?

- Do you think that the teacher has a responsibility to know more about the cultural background of her students?

John H. Bodley: *"Creating Nunavut"*

In class you learned that Nunavut is the largest land claim settlement in favor of native peoples anywhere/ ever. In 1999 the residents of this area voted to become a new self-governing Territory in Canada. The Inuit make up 85% of the total population (a little over 80,000) of Nunavut and play major roles in both government and business.

- What does "Nunavut" mean in the Inuit language?

- Bodley writes that Nunavut is about the size of this country?

- What is the political status of Nunavut in Canada?

- How do the goals listed for the future of Nunavut compare to goals for native peoples in Mankiller's article?

- What economic development potential for Nunavut was mentioned in class but not in the article? Why?

Leonard Little Finger: *"We Walk on Our Ancestors: The Sacredness of the Black Hills"*

Many Americans have visited the Black Hills in South Dakota to see Mount Rushmore, but it is also a sacred site for Indians. This article addresses a lot of the issues that we have been introduced to in this section: the importance of sacred sites to indigenous peoples, the violation of treaty rights, the control of resources, and even assimilation.

- Why are the Black Hills sacred to the Lakota?

- What discovery led to an attempt to renegotiate the treaties of 1851 and 1868? Were they renegotiated?

- Why does Little Finger worry about the impact of assimilation on the Black Hills?

- Would you label Little Finger as XY or Z? Why?

FILM REPORT

The American Experience: In the White Man's Image

- What is the main idea of this video?

- List important facts used to support the main idea.

- How does this video relate to your readings and the lecture?

PRACTICE TEST QUESTIONS

Multiple Choice

1. The most politically correct term for Indigenous Peoples in our country and Canada today is
   a. Indians
   b. American Indians
   c. First Nation Peoples
   d. Native Americans
   e. Indigenous People with Tribal Rights

2. Native Americans make up less than 1 percent of the U.S. population.
   a. true
   b. false

3. These three Indian crops/foods now make up 60 percent of the food consumed in the world today.
   a. potato, tobacco, tomato
   b. coffee, cocoa, llama milk
   c. manioc, maize, potato
   d. cranberries, turkeys, squash
   e. pumpkins, corn, rice

4. Russell Means would be classified as a(n) _____ by William Hodges.
   a. X
   b. country Indian
   c. Z
   d. Y
   e. MacIntosh

5. The goal of the microbe that causes epidemic disease is to kill off its host population.
   a. true
   b. false

6. Which of the following is NOT a myth or stereotype about Indians
   a. Most Indians do not drink
   b. Indians are a vanishing race
   c. Indians get special privileges
   d. Native Americans prefer to be called Native American
   e. American Indians are easily identifiable

Matching

7. _____ Culture area

8. _____ Adaptation

9. _____ Saynday

10. _____ Paternalism

11. _____ BIA

a. Bureau of Indian Affairs or Bureau of Idiots Anonymous, depending on your perspective.

b. A geographic region in which there existed a number of societies following similar patterns of life.

c. U.S. Indian policy based on the assumption that the Indian is biologically equal to whites, but is culturally inferior.

d. Kiowa hero uncle.

e. The process by which groups become fitted physically and culturally to particular environments over several generations.

Short Answer

1. What discoveries have led to new theories about the original migrations of people to the Americas.

2. Define the concept of "culture area". Who developed this concept? Why?

3. In the XYZ grouping, which group is the most numerous? (In addition to giving the letter, describe the group.)

4. What is the source of the stereotypes About Native Americans? Explain.

5. Relate Indian Gaming to the assimilation policies of the 1950's.

Essay

1. Captain Richard Pratts slogan was "kill the Indian in him and save the man" Does this Refer to genocide or Assimilation? Why? What role do both of these play in the myth of the vanishing Indian?

2. Write a letter to the editor in response to Andy Rooney's article. (Be sure to show how much better educated you are about Native Americans than he is.)

3. Discuss the pros and cons of the policies of assimilation and pluralism. Which policy do you support? Why?

4. How does the article "An Indian Father's Plea" relate to the Native American Inventory? (Relate to more than one point.)

5. At the beginning of Unit II, I told you that many Native Americans prefer to be called "First Nations Peoples." Please explain why.

6. What role did disease play in the conquest of the New World? Be sure to include both cultural and biological adaptation in your answer. Use both the human point of view and the "bugs" point of view.

7. Relate Little Finger's article about the Black Hills to the following concepts talked about in class: rights to practice your culture (religion), treaty violations and court cases, culture change and assimilation.

LECTURE OUTLINE—SOUTH AMERICA

I. Geography and culture areas (pre-contact)

                                                     *Map IIa

  A. Grasslands
      1. Foraging—Hunting and gathering
      2. Band form of social organization
      3. Yahgan

  B. Amazon River Basin—Lowlands
      1. Horticulture—Slash and burn
         a. Manioc
         b. Peanuts
      2. Tribe and chiefdom
      3. Kayapo
      4. Yanomamo   *Film
      5. Shavante   *Maybury-Lewis

  C. Andes Mountain—Highlands
      1. Intensive agriculture
         a. Irrigation and terracing
         b. Domesticated animals
             1) Camelids
            2) Turkeys
            3) Bees
            4) Guinea pigs
         c. High Altitude Crops
            1) Potato
            2) Quinoa
      2. State societies
         3) Inca

II. Culture areas after contact

  A. Onion model

  B. Grasslands
      1. Immigration and genocide
      2. Ranching

C. Lowlands
1. Portuguese and Spanish
2. Major rivers/minor rivers
3. Isolation
4. Gold, settlement programs, cattle herding

D. Highlands
1. Closed corporate communities
2. Encomienda system
3. Hacienda system
   a. Patron
   b. Peon
   c. Paternalism
4. Land reforms
   a. Latifundia
   b. Minifundia

KEY TERMS AND VOCABULARY

Andes Mountains

Amazon

Rain forest

Grasslands

Foraging

Horticulture

Agriculture

Quinoa

Manioc

Hacienda

Minifundia

Latifundia

Patron

Paternalism

Peon

Peonage

Share-cropping

Closed corporate community

Onion model

Band

Tribe

Chiefdom

State

Nomadic

Egalitarian

GROUPS YOU SHOULD KNOW

Yanomamo

Shavante

Yahgan

Kayapo

Inca/Inka

Map IIC
Geographical and Cultural Areas of South America

CHART IIB   Distincitve Features of Three Cultural Areas of South America

Area	Type of Social Organization	Subsistence Level	Typical Crops
Grasslands (Yahgan)	Band	Foraging	None
Lowlands (Yanomamo) (Kayapo)	Tribe/chiefdom	Horticulture	Manioc Peanuts Banana
Highlands (Inca)	State	Agriculture	Squash Potato Quinoa

ARTICLE REVIEWS

Pia Maybury-Lewis: *"One Step Forward—Two Steps Back"*

Maybury-Lewis made two trips to Brazil to visit the Shavante Indians. Twenty-four years separated her two trips. During that time many changes had occured due to the effects of modernization.

- What are some of the changes that Maybury-Lewis observes?

- Has change affected both men and women in the same manner? Explain.

- Do you think that perhaps changes in our own society from 1958 to 1982 had any role in Maybury-Lewis's observations? Explain.

PRACTICE TEST QUESTIONS

Multiple Choice

1. The highest level of political organization found in pre-contact South America was:
   a. chiefdom.
   b. state.
   c. tribe.
   d. band.
   e. nomads

2. Latifundia are:
   a. fields along the banks of the Amazon that flood annually, leaving several inches of new topsoil.
   b. the local political organization for the Shuar tribal governments.
   c. llamas kept for milking.
   d. freeze-dried potatoes.
   e. none of the above.

3. Between her two visits, Pia Maybury-Lewis observed that the condition of women among the Shavante had improved with more Western acculturation.
   a. true
   b. false

4. Age groups are an essential mechanism for organizing political action in this culture.
   a. Kayapo
   b. Yahgan
   c. Inca
   d. Haida
   e. Fuegians

5. The Onion Model predicts what will happen to a native culture after contact. What part of culture does it focus on?
   a. economic system
   b. political organization
   c. geographical factors
   d. religion and morality
   e. all of the above

6. _____ is similar to the system of sharecropping that replaced slavery in the United States after the Civil War.
   a. debt peonage
   b. patron peonage
   c. peasant paternalism
   d. chattel slavery
   e. age grades

Matching

Map of South America

7. _____ Grasslands
8. _____ State societies
9. _____ Lowlands
10. _____ No farming
11. _____ Andes Mountains
12. _____ Yahgan
13. _____ Shavante
14. _____ Inka

Short Answer

1. Who are the Shavante? How have they changed in recent years?

2. What are the three geographical and cultural areas of South America?

3. Which culture area had the best chance of surviving spanish colonialism?

Essay

1. What are the three cultural/geographical areas of South America? Draw a map. Explain their environmental adaptations, their subsistence patterns, and their levels of political development.
2. What is the Onion Model of social change? Draw a chart of the model. How does it apply in South America?
3. What new dimension of culture contact is addressed on Maybury-Lewis's Article? What impact did the feminist movement have? On the Author? On Anthropology? On the Shavante?

REVIEW FOR QUIZ #2—NORTH AMERICA AND SOUTH AMERICA

Bering Straits and migration

Indian awareness inventory and stereotypes

**Andy Rooney—What his article illustrates
.8 percent**

Navajo

Culture area

Adaptation

Pluralism

Assimilation—Forced assimilation

Directed acculturation

Training schools

BIA, AIM

Red power, radish: Apple

Mestizo

Peyote

Manioc

Maize

Potato

How Indians differ from other minorities

XYZ

Basic assumptions of U.S. Indian policy

Health problems

Education

Indian Education Act of 1972

***Winds of Change,* issues in Indian Sovereignty**

Nunavut

Percaps

South America

**Map of South America: Three cultural/
geographical areas; major crops types of
culture for each area; historical/present**

Minifundia/latifundia

Patron/peon

Closed corporate community

Encomienda system

Hacienda system

Groups for N.A. and S.A.

Shavante

Lumbee

Penobscot

Articles

Yanomamo

Aztecs

Incas/Inka

Kayapo

Passamaquoddy

Navaho

UNIT III

AFRICA AND OCEANIA

OVERVIEW

The Europeans benefited greatly from the discovery and colonization of the New World. Eventually they began to turn their attention to the potential wealth in other parts of the world. To satisfy the demand for labor in the New World, the Europeans turned to the slave trade in Africa. In 1501 the Spanish colonists in the New World were granted permission from King and Queen to be allowed to import slaves from Africa. The development of the colonies would not have been possible without African labor. The colonists in needed both African labor and expertise. At the beginning of industrialization, Europeans looked to Africa as a potential source of raw materials and markets for manufactured goods. The European countries all felt that they were entitled to a piece of the African continent, and they raced against each other to explore it, claim it, and colonize it. The colonial period was short lived in Africa, but it had an impact. We will explore the influence of European colonization and the expansion of the religions of Islam and Christianity on traditional Africa.

In Oceania, we will study the themes of diversity, migration, and European influence. Oceania not only had a wealth of resources, but it was strategically important during World War II and the Cold War. The United States has played a neo-colonial role in this area. Anthropology has also played an active role in this period. It has been used to support both colonialism and native rights.

LECTURE OUTLINE—AFRICA

I. Introduction to Africa

    A. Stereotypes of Africa
        1. Uncivilized
        2. Mostly jungle
        3. Life is dangerous
        4. Exotic cultural practices

    B. Why study peoples and cultures of Africa?
        1. Cradle of civilization
        2. Human evolution
        3. Ancestral home of one out of eight Americans
        4. Linguistic diversity
        5. Strategic to world development
        6. Social problems

    C. Africa's triple heritage (Ali Mazrui)
        1. Traditional Africa
        2. Islam—Arabs
        3. Colonialism—Europeans

    D. Maps
        1. Geographical Areas
        2. African Nationalism
        3. Current issues

II. Four major sources for change in Africa

    A. Slave Trade
        1. Arab slave trade
        2. European slave trade
            a. demand for labor in the New World
            b. slavery and warfare
            c. population decline
            d. loss of skilled labor
            e. racism
            f. slavery in the modern world

    B. Missions
        1. Islam
        2. Christian
            a. ethnocentrism
            b. partnership with colonial governments

      3. Rhodesia

         a. Cecil Rhodes

         b. Zulu Wars

         c. Gatling Gun

C. European Colonialsim/Industrial Revolution   *Cronk

    1. Scramble for Africa

    2. 1884 Conference in Germany

      a. colonial carve-up

         1. Senegal and Zambia

    3. How Europeans extracted wealth from Africa

      a. Raw materials

      b. Markets

      c. Land and settlers

         1. direct rule

         2. indirect rule

         3. French assimilation policy

      d. Head tax

      e. Forced labor

         1. chibaro

         2. Belgian Congo/Mozambique

      f. Cash crops

    4. Italian invasion 1935

D. Capitalism

    1. formal economy

    2. informal economy

      a. Jua Kali

      b. Zambia

VII. Africa today

A. Problems in Africa

    1. AIDS

    2. Corruption

    3. Low GNP and poverty

    4. Warfare

B. African solutions to African problems

VIII. Pastoralism in Africa

A. Pastoralism today

    1. Transhumance

B. Pastoralists and colonization

    1. Awlad' Ali   *Abu-Lughad

IX. Education

  A. Hausa-Nigeria   *Schildkrout

  B. Gîkûyû-Kenya   *Thiongo

KEY TERMS AND VOCABULARY

Temperate climate

Kwame Nkrumah—African Nationalism

Islam

Muslim

Africa's Triple Heritage

Ali Mazrui

Colonial Carve-Up Conference of 1884

Ottoman Empire

Ethiopia/Liberia

American Colonial Society

Mauritania/Sudan

African Union

Bakseesh, Dash, Long Legs

Heterogeneity

Capitalism

Multilingual

Apartheid

Gatling gun

Factors, factories, slavery

Cecil Rhodes

Zulu

Direct rule

Indirect rule

Black Frenchmen

Head tax

Chibaro

Cash crops

Abyssinia

Zambia

AIDS

Jua Kali

Formal economy/informal economy

Purdah

Pastoralism

Plan B

GROUPS YOU SHOULD KNOW—AFRICA

Bedouins

Awlad' Ali

Gîkûyû

Bushman, San, !Kung, Khoikhoi, Ju/'hoansi

Lost Boys

Hausa

Maasai/Masai

Mukogoda

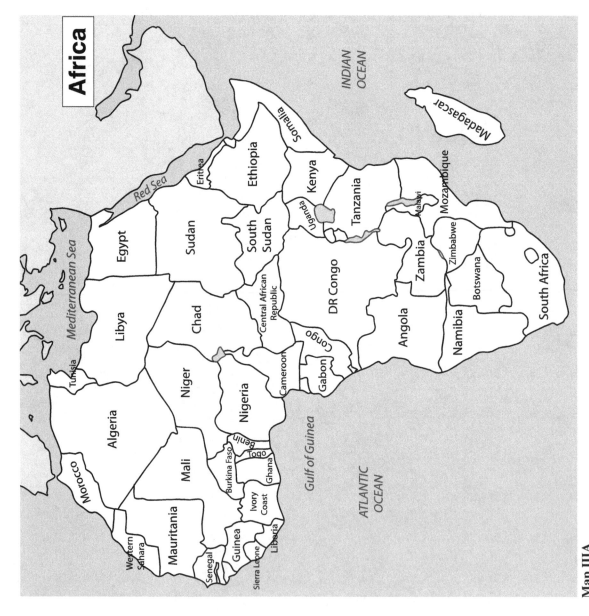

Map IIIA
© pavalena/Shutterstock.com

ARTICLE REVIEWS

Lila Abu-Lughad: *"Change and the Egyptian Bedouin"*

This is an account of a group of people who have adapted to modernization and culture change and still manage to maintain their cultural identity. They have managed to circumvent the attempts of the Egyptian government to change their culture.

- What attempts to change the culture has the government of Egypt made?

- How have the Awlad' Ali gotten around these programs?

- What is the most important thing to a Bedouin? How do you get it?

- How does the above lead to a strong cultural identity?

Ngugi wa Thiongo: *"Decolonizing the Mind"*

Thiongo writes about his experience as a young Kenyan of the Gîkûyû tribe who goes to an English school. He is proud of his culture and heritage, but the English school does not acknowledge that. Not only did the school teach him the English language and English culture, but it also tried to teach him that their language and culture was superior to his own.

- What methods were used to teach the African children in the English school?

- How did the school system support colonialism?

- What do you think that Thiongo means by the phrase, "decolonizing the mind"?

- Relate Thiongo's experience to those of young Native Americans during the boarding school era.

Lee Cronk and Beth Leech: *"Where's Koisia?"*

The Mukogoda were once cave dwelling hunters and gatherers living in Kenya in East Africa. In the last five decades they have experienced very rapid and almost complete cultural change. The article explores both the impact of Fagan's ripple effect and applied anthropology.

- How did the contact of the Europeans and the Maasai impact their neighbors, the Mukogoda?

- What role did Bride Price play in culture change?

- Why weren't the two developments projects, the garden project and the water project unsuccessful?

- Who is Koisa?

Enid Schildkrout: *"Schooling or Seclusion"*

This is a different article about education and its effect on society. A new education program is offering educational opportunities to both boys and girls among the Hausa of Northern Nigeria. This program has affected the sexes differently.

- What is Purdah? How is it practiced by the Hausa?

- How does schooling impact the ability of married women to run their businesses?

- Does education improve the life of a Hausa woman?

- What does the article tell us about our values toward education?

- Does Schildkrout argue that education for women is bad?

PRACTICE TEST QUESTIONS

Multiple Choice

1. Africa is:
   a. mostly jungle.
   b. twice as large as the United States.
   c. heterogenous.
   d. ruled by witch doctors and superstition.
   e. a continent bordered by the Pacific and the Indian Ocean.

2. The 1884 Conference:
   a. is sometimes referred to as the Scramble for Africa.
   b. took place in Germany.
   c. was a meeting of representatives from European countries who divided up Africa among themselves.
   d. was attended by people who thought that they were going to help Africa by colonizing it.
   e. all of the above.

3. There is documentation that chattel slavery, the buying and selling of human beings, still exists in some countries in Africa.
   a. true
   b. false

4. The French practiced a policy of assimilation in their African colonies. This meant that they tried to make _____ of the people living there.
   a. slaves
   b. bourgeoisie
   c. Native Americans
   d. Black Frenchmen
   e. Tante Sallies

5. Forced labor in Africa was called:
   a. corvée.
   b. chibaro.
   c. mita.
   d. indentured servitude.
   e. mikiri.

6. An indirect means of forcing labor was:
   a. slavery.
   b. the women's market.
   c. sitting on a man.
   d. kidnapping people to work on building the railroads.
   e. the head tax.

7. When Zambia became independent from Great Britain in 1964, it appeared to have a bright future because it had:
   a. a strong stable government.
   b. the world's second largest copper mines.
   c. billions of dollars in foreign reserves.
   d. tremendous agricultural potential.
   e. all of the above.

8. The informal sector of the economy in Africa:
    a. is not counted in the GNP.
    b. is inventive and successful.
    c. is called the Jua Kali.
    d. is often more productive than the formal economy.
    e. all of the above.

9. The article by Thiongo, "Decolonizing the Mind," should remind you of the Carlisle School experience of:
    a. the Gîkûyû.
    b. the white Kenyans.
    c. Native Americans.
    d. the typical British public school system.
    e. Black African university graduates.

Matching

10. _____ Egypt
11. _____ Liberia
12. _____ Sudan
13. _____ South Africa
14. _____ Nigeria

a. Allegedly still practicing slavery.
b. Never colonized.
c. Home of the Awlad' Ali.
d. Last country in Africa to achieve successful participation of Blacks in government.
e. Home of the Hausa.

Short Answer

1. Explain the statement "There is no such thing as a typical African."

2. Explain how the Mukogodo of Kenya were impacted by colonialism when they did not experience direct contact with the Europeans?

3. Explain the difference between formal and informal economies. How do these concepts relate to Africa?

4. What does Mazrui mean by the phrase, "African solutions to African problems"? List some examples.

Essay

1. What happened in Zambia after its independence in the 1960s? Is this typical of what happened in other African countries?
2. Using Thiongo's article on his educational experience, compare it to that of Native Americans in the past and today.
3. What methods did Europeans use to extract wealth from Africa?
4. What are the sources of many of the stereotypes that Americans have of Africa?
5. Explain the difference between informal and formal economies? Make up an example.
6. What is the impact of AIDS on sub-Saharan Africa? Are there any simple solutions to this problem? Explain.

LECTURE OUTLINE—OCEANIA

I. What is Oceania?

    A. Geography
        1. 1/8 world's surface
        2. 20,000 to 30,000 islands
            a. Volcanic islands
            b. Coral reef islands
                1) Atolls
            c. Archipelagos

    B. Culture—three culture areas
        1. Melanesia—Black islands   *Sorenson
        2. Polynesia—Many islands
        3. Micronesia—Small islands

    C. Themes of Oceania
        1. Diversity
        2. Migrations
        3. 400 years of European contact

II. Historical experience

    A. Discovery
        1. Spanish
        2. Captain Cook

    B. Trade with China
        1. Sandalwood
        2. Sea cucumbers

    C. Plantations
        1. Copra
        2. Pineapples
        3. Sugar

III. Traits characteristic of all culture areas

    A. Agricultural and fishing

    B. Social systems based on kinship and village

    C. Strong sea-going orientation

IV. Culture Areas of Oceania

    A. Polynesia
        1. Noble Savage
        2. Chiefdoms

    B. Micronesia
        1. Breadfruit
        2. Swamp taro

    C. Melanesia
        1. Big Man
        2. Warfare

V. Current Political status

    A. Changing statuses

    B. Independence
        1. Iran Java
        2. PNG

    C. Neocolonialism
        1. Trust Territories
        2. U.N. Strategic Rental

    D. Nuclear Testing

IV. Examples of contemporary issues in Oceania

    A. Melanesia
        1. New Caledonia: The French
            a. History
            b. Kanaks
            c. Independence movements
            d. referendums
        2. Fiji: The English
            a. History
            b. Fijians and Indians
            c. Coups

B. Polynesia
1. New Zealand
   a. History
   b. Maori and Pakeha
   c. Backwards Acculturation
2. Tahiti

C. Micronesia
1. History
2. Impact of U.S. stewardship
   a. Health
      1) Suicide rates
      2) Infant health
      3) Radiation sickness
      4) Tobacco and alcohol
   b. Education
   c. Changing lifestyles for women
      1) availability of birth control

KEY TERMS AND VOCABULARY

Oceania

Atoll

Coral Reef Island

Volcanic Island

Archipelago

Polynesia

Micronesia

Melanesia

Papua New Guinea

Irian Java/West Papua

Stratified chiefdom

Hierarchy

Pantheon

Mana

Tapu

Blood magic

Noble savage

Big Men

Sorcery

Copra

Redistribution

New Zealand

Hawaii

New Caledonia

Fiji

Tante Sally/ Aunt Sally

Strategic rental

Cargo cults

Neo-colonialism

Pakeha

Backwards-acculturation

Moko

GROUPS YOU SHOULD KNOW

Kanaks

Maori

Tahitians

Fijians

Fore

OCEANIA

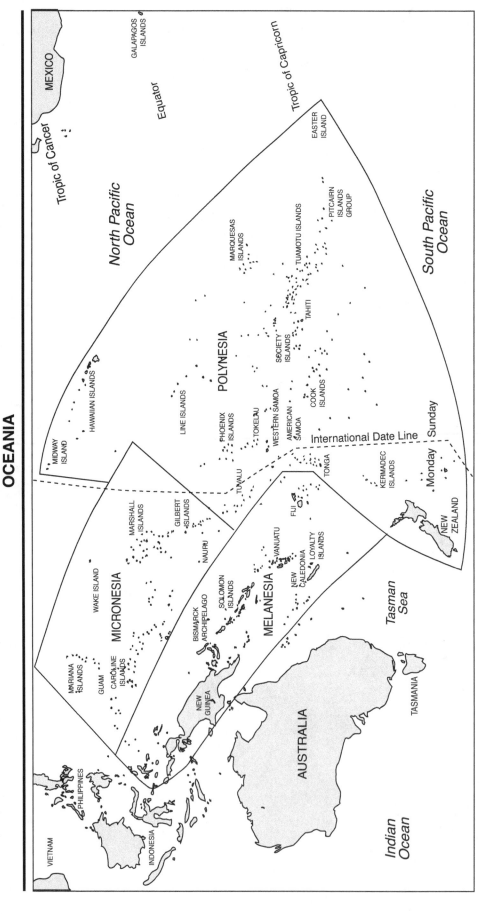

Map IIIB

The Three Main Pacific Island Groups

The Pacific Islands can be divided into three main groups: (1) Melanesia, meaning *black islands*; (2) Micronesia, meaning *small islands*; and (3) Polynesia, meaning *many islands*. This grouping is based on the race and customs of the native peoples and on the islands' geography.

WORLD BOOK map

ARTICLE REVIEWS

Richard Sorenson: *"Growing Up as a Fore is to be 'In Touch' and Free"*

The Fore are native peoples of New Guinea. Living in the interior of the island, they have had little contact until recently. When Sorenson arrived in the highlands in 1963, they had already begun to change. He attributes rapid change among the Fore to their traditional childrearing practices.

- How does Sorenson relate childrearing customs to the rapid culture change Among the Fore? What does he mean when he refers to their "Achiles Heel"?

- What are the similarities and differences of the "walk-about" for the Fore and Australian Aborigines?

- What dies Sorenson say about the negative effects of globalization?

- Do you think that he idealizes the traditional Fore way of life?

PRACTICE TEST QUESTIONS

Be able to identify the following on a map page 85:

The Pacific Ocean
Australia
Three cultural areas of Oceania
New Guinea—Papua New Guinea and Irian Java (West Papua)
New Zealand
Tasmania

Multiple Choice

1. This nation is known as the Tante Sally of the Pacific.
   a. France
   b. Great Britain
   c. France
   d. Indonesia
   e. Australia

2. In the 16th and 17th centuries many European philosophers viewed "primitive" peoples as:
   a. noble savages.
   b. beautiful and simple people.
   c. communistic.
   d. 10-year old children.
   e. all of the above.

3. According to Sorenson, what is the "Achille's Heel" of the Fore?
   a. coffee plantations
   b. roads and railroads
   c. a childrearing system that produces a person that is confident, independent, and willing to explore new things
   d. culture shock
   e. a market economy

4. This large island is occupied by two countries.
   a. Hawaii
   b. New Zealand
   c. Australia
   d. New Guinea
   e. New Caledonia

5. Oceania includes all of the islands in the Pacific Ocean.
   a. true
   b. false

6. This group provides an example of backwards-acculturation.
   a. Maori
   b. Kanaks
   c. Marquesans
   d. Dani
   e. Ekari

7. France conducted below-ground nuclear testing on these islands in the Fall of 1995.
   a. New Caledonia
   b. Cook Islands
   c. Tasmania
   d. Tahiti
   e. France signed a nuclear test ban treaty in 1965, and has done no testing since then.

8. The first area of Oceania to be settled by humans was
   a. Melanesia
   b. Tahiti
   c. Polynesia
   d. the Carteret islands
   e. the Hawaiian Islands

9. The culture area with the smallest amount of land and the least people is:
   a. Australia.
   b. Melanesia.
   c. Micronesia.
   d. Polynesia.
   e. Indonesia.

Short Answer

1. What is the difference between a volcanic island and coral reef island? What does this mean in terms of human occupation?

2. What islands of the Pacific Ocean are not considered part of Oceania?

3. List three common "themes" in Oceania.

4. What is strategic rental?

5. What is breadfruit? Why is it considered the "perfect food" for human beings? What role will it play in the global future?

Essay

1. What are the basic differences between the goals and methods of anthropologists and missionaries?

2. What are the three culture areas of Oceania? List their cultural and geographical attributes. (You may do this in chart form.)

	Geographical	Cultural
Area 1		
Area 2		
Area 3		

3. Why are the French called the Tante Sally of the Pacific?

4. Compare the French in New Caledonia to the English in Fiji.

5. What is the concept of the "noble savage"? Do you think that anthropologists are victims of the concept today? Why? Why not?

6. List some of the negative impacts of a strong U.S. influence in Micronesia.

7. Explain the connection between nuclear testing and the Pacific from the 1940s to the 1990s.

REVIEW FOR QUIZ 3—AFRICA AND OCEANIA

Main goal of Europeans in Africa / how accomplished

Compare British, French, Belgian, and Portuguese colonial systems

1935—what Italy did? impact?

Africa—continent with over 50 countries

Heterogeneity, Triple Heritage, typical African?

Ali Mazrui

Islam / Muslim

Linguistic Diversity

1884 Conference in Germany—Scramble for Africa

How Europeans regard Africans, racism

Methods that the Europeans used to extract wealth from Africa

Racism	**Chibaro**	**Awlad'Ali**	**Maasai**
Paternalism	**Transhumance**	**Bedouin**	
Apartheid		**AIDS**	

Missionaries—goals / methods / actual accomplishments

Zulu wars

Gatling Gun

Reasons to study Africa / stereotypes of Africa

Indirect rule / direct rule

Black Frenchmen

Pastoralists

Zambia, Jua Kali, formal economy, informal economy

Educational and assimilation—Thiongo, Hausa

Maasai and Mukogodo

Map—Three cultural areas of Oceania

Concept of noble savage and primitives in 16th- and 17th-century literature of Pacific contact

Cpts Wallis, Cook, and Bougainville

Industrial Revolution and displacement of European population

Maori—culture, terms, missionaries

Chiefdoms

Big Man

Elite Maori

Backwards acculturation

U.S. territories

Fore

East Papua/West Papua

Strategic rental

U.N. Trust Territories

Problems in Micronesia

Nuclear testing

New Caledonia—Kanaks

Fiji—Colonialism, Indians, tourism

Tahiti—native culture, relations to French

Tante Sally

Missionaries and culture

UNIT IV

CONCLUSION:
TASMANIA, AUSTRALIA, JAPAN AND COURSE REVIEW

OVERVIEW

In this final unit of the course, I want to examine two very different contact events and outcomes. In one a group of people and their culture became extinct and in the other the people and their culture have global prominence and are have become one of the world's wealthiest and most powerful countries. This also gives us the opportunity to include the two continents, Asia and Australia, in our course.

The most rapid and complete case of genocide in contact history took place on the island of Tasmania. A whole group of people, the Tasmanian Aborigines, were wiped out in roughly three generations of contact British settlers. We will compare and contrast the settlement policies of the British in Tasmania and those in Australia. Modern Australian Aborigines have a lot in common with contemporary Native Americans, thus bringing us "full circle" in our course.

I have also included a section on Japan in this last unit. The history of relations between the West and Japan does not follow the pattern that we have seen repeating itself so often. The Japanese decided early after contact that the Westerners were the barbarians and they effectively kept us out of their country for more than two centuries. Once contact was re-established, events proceeded quite differently, Japan modernized by borrowing heavily from the West, but at the same time remaining distinctly Japanese.

The focus of the entire course from the first day to the last, has been on culture contact and it's global impact in the both past and the present. We have looked at European expansion from the Age of Discovery Age of Discovery right into modern times. For most of us westerners, we have only learned one side of this story. By now you should be aware of the changes in our own culture that has been a product of this contact. Hopefully we have also developed an ability to see an event from multiple perspectives and will become more aware of our own ethnocentrism.

Finally, we will return to the role that anthropology can and does play in helping people to improve their lives. Anthropologists, with their cross-cultural training, holistic perspective, and experience living in other cultures, are well-suited to dealing with culture contact and it's subsequent changes and they are now playing a much greater role in world events. We will look at some of the failures and successes of applied anthropologists as they attempt to help improve the lives of people here and abroad.

LECTURE OUTLINE—TASMANIA, AUSTRALIA, JAPAN AND COURSE REVIEW

I. Tasmania

    A. The Tasmanian Extinction
        1. genocide
        2. Truganini
        3. Australia   *Cheater
           a. Terra Nullius
           b. Lost Generations
        4. Genocide in 20th Century
        5. genocide today

II. Japan

    A. Japanese popular culture   *Condry
        1. J-POP

    B. What you know from class
        1. World map
        2. Sushi
        3. First World
        4. Expansion history

    C. Europe in Asia
        1. Imperialism
        2. Trade
           a. Maritime power
           b. Commerce
           c. Missions

    D. Early history of Japan
        1. Jomon
        2. Ainu

    E. The Shogunate
        1. Portuguese
        2. Dutch
        3. Jesuits

    F. Over 200 Years of Isolation

    G. Modernization
        1. Commodore Perry
        2. Meiji Restoration

        a. Trade
        b. Idealistic nationalism
        c. Education
        d. Industrialization
        e. Imperialism

  H. WWII
     1. <u>Chrysanthemum and the Sword</u>
     2. US occupation
     3. Article 9
     4. "Nuclear allergy"

III. Review of the semester

  A. Study of the expansion of European states
     1. Greenland and the Crusades
     2. Neo-Europes
         a. Temperate climates

  B. What happened at contact?
     1. Friendly trade
     2. Acculturation
     3. Disease
         a. Virgin soil epidemics
         b. Historical epidemiology
     4. Slavery
     5. Reservations/segregation and relocation
     6. Genocide

  C. Aboriginal resistance
     1. War
         a. Native Americans
         b. Zulu
     2. Spiritual resistance—revitalization movements
         a. Ghost dance
         b. Handsome Lake
         c. Cargo cults
         d. Christianity

  D. Assimilation

  E. Pluralism

  F. Agency

III. Development issues
    A. Modernization theory
        1. Assumptions of modernization theory
        2. Is it possible?   *Bodley
            a. Cultural factors
            b. Human population
            c. Resource shortages
            d. Energy crisis

    B. Foreign aid
        1. World rankings
        2. US AID
        3. UN
        4. NGO's
        5. Microfinancing

    C. Arms race and development

IV. Applied anthropology
        1. Case studies

    A. Successes

    B. Limitations

V. Course goals
    1. Students' perspective
    2. Understanding globalism

KEY TERMS AND VOCABULARY

Genocide

Lost Generation

Terra Nullius

Shogunate

Meiji Restoration

Hip Hop

Tasmania

Ethnocide/genocide

Neo-Europes

Temperate climate

Virgin soil epidemics

Historical epidemiology

US AID

NGO

Peace Corps

"Standard of Living"

"Diseases of Development"

Malnutrition

Ecocide

Agency/plan B

Christine Cheater: *"Stolen Girlhood: Australia's Assimilation Policies and Aboriginal Girls."*

This article offers a close-up look at the experience of half caste aboriginal girls who were taken from their homes and parents and placed in boarding schools. These girls were part of an assimilation program and made up a significant portion of Australia's "Lost Generations".

- What method does the author use to acquire her data for the article?

- This article focuses on girls that were removed from their families. Why girls and not boys?

- What is meant by the term. half caste? How were half caste individuals treated differently than full-bloods? Why?

- What are some of the ways that boarding school girls used to cope with the stress that they were under?

Ian Condry: *"Japanese Hip Hop and the Globalization of Popular Culture"*

This subject of this article is the diffusion of American Hip Hop music to Japan. The author did fieldwork in Hip Hop clubs in Tokyo and studied many other parts of the music business. Condry looks at both the global and local aspects of the borrowing of popular culture.

- How does the information in this article illustrate the two parts of the definition of diffusion?

- What is meant by a "new hybrid cultural form"? How does Japanese Hip Hop fit this description?

- Discuss the concepts of individualism and groupism as they relate to the adoption of Hip Hop in Japan.

- What happened at New Year's Eve at one of the clubs?

John Bodley: *"The Price of Progress"*

By now you should realize that modernization and development are not always to the benefit of Fourth World peoples. Bodley goes through a list documenting this observation. He names lots of peoples and places: you should focus on issues.

- What is meant by the phrase "standard of living"? Is it an ethnocentric concept?

- What have been some of the negative aspects of modernization and development for Fourth World peoples?

- Does Bodley offer any solutions to these problems?

- Why do you think I have chosen this article to be the last assignment in the course.

PRACTICE TEST QUESTIONS

Multiple Choice

1. The Japanese categorize their social relationships into two sets of pairs. These pairs directly influence all social and business relationships. What are they?
   a. foreigner/native and circle/square
   b. male/female and dominant/submissive
   c. frames/windows and doors/arches
   d. Gaijin/Nippon and Japanese/American
   e. insider/outsider and front/rear

2. What does Condry mean to say when he uses the phrase "Traveling against the mainstream"?
   a. Japanese Hip Hop fans are too individualistic for Japanese cultural values
   b. Japanese Hip Hop is very different from American Hip Hop
   c. Hip Hop as a musical form arose to protest the values of mainstream American society
   d. Japanese clubbers are riding the trains to the clubs when everyone else is heading home or going to work
   e. globalization conflicts with localization

3. Bodley documents how the health improves and the standard of living gets better for Fourth World people after contact.
   a. true
   b. false

4. Historical epidemiologists study diseases of the past. They use information from:
   a. virgin soil epidemics that are occurring today.
   b. historical records.
   c. archaeological evidence
   d. ancient human remains.
   e. all of the above.

5. The following is a very popular Japanese cultural export. It is a type of comic book.
   a. anime
   b. sushi
   c. manga
   d. J-POPS
   e. J-COMS

Short Answer

1. Relate the following—Plan B, Agency, Indigenous people.

2. What is a Neo-Europe? Where are they most likely to be found? Give an example.

3. List four ways that the standard of living for Fourth World peoples has declined.

4. Ian Condry attended a New Year's Eve party in Tokyo's Harlem. When the clock struck 12, the clubbers wished each other a happy new year. What was notable about this event?

5. What ideals are spread by Hip Hop in Japan? How is this contrary to traditional Japanese culture?

Essay

1. What is applied anthropology? In what areas has it been most effective? Explain using examples.
2. Sometimes the result of contact was aboriginal resistance. What are its two forms? Give examples of each. What was the long-term outcome?
3. What role does Applied Anthropology play in movements like Plan B? Give examples?
4. "The most seriously threatening contacts for people today are between indigenous peoples and their neighbors in the increasing conflict over rights to land and resources". Relate this quote to Fagan's concepts of the "clash of cultures" and the ripple effect.
5. What does Bodley mean when he states that the "standard of living" is an ethnocentric concept? Does the "standard of living" for Fourth World peoples always improve after contact? Give examples.

6. What are "virgin soil epidemics"? How are they related to history? What impact have they had? What impact are they having now? Should AIDS be considered a virgin soil epidemic?

7. What events over a 50 year period resulted in the Tasmanian Extinction?

8. Explain the reasons that there were a disproportionate number of girls sent to boarding schools and/or adopted in the Australian assimilation program.

REVIEW FOR QUIZ #4—CONCLUSION: TASMANIA, AUSTRALIA, JAPAN AND COURSE REVIEW

Tasmania

Tasmanian Extinction

genocide

Truganini

Lost Generation

Terra Nullius

Native Police

Japan

J-POP

Imperialism, commerce

Maritime expertise and control of trades routes

Jomon and Ainu

Shogunate, 200 years of isolation

1853 Perry

Meiji Restoration

Chrysanthemum and the Sword

Article 9

Japan

Early history

The Shogunate

Portuguese

Jesuits

Isolation

Modernization

Meiji Restoration

Trade

Commodore Perry

WWII

Today

Popular culture

Expansion of European States—Successes and failures

Neo-Europes

Virgin soil epidemics

Genocide, ethnocide

Ghost dance, cargo cults

Modernization theory

Applied anthropology

First, Second, Third, Fourth World

Pluralism / assimilation

Standard of living

Average per capita income in Third World

Population 7.5 billion/predicted to be 8.9 by 2050

Failed development projects